# UP ALL NIGHT!
## NOCTURNAL ANIMALS

# OWLS
## at Night

Kathleen A. Klatte

**PowerKiDS** press
New York

Published in 2021 by The Rosen Publishing Group, Inc.
29 East 21st Street, New York, NY 10010

Portions of this work were originally authored by Doreen Gonzales and published as *Owls in the Dark*. All new material in this edition was authored by Kathleen A. Klatte.

Editor: Kathleen Klatte
Book Design: Michael Flynn

Photo Credits: Cover Javier Chiavone/Shutterstock.com; (series background) MoreThanPicture/Shutterstock.com; p. 4 Alan Tunnicliffe/Shutterstock.com; p. 5 BMJ/Shutterstock.com; p. 7 hutch photography/Shutterstock.com; p. 9 FJAH/Shutterstock.com; p. 10 Richard Whitcombe/Shutterstock.com; p. 11 Patrick Rolands/Shutterstock.com; p. 12 Dusan Vainer/Shutterstock.com; p. 13 Kevin Farr Foto/Shutterstock.com; p. 15 Todd Maertz/Shutterstock.com; p. 17 moosehenderson/Shutterstock.com; p. 18 Chris Hill/Shutterstock.com; p. 19 Emily Nestlerode/Shutterstock.com; p. 21 mlorenz/Shutterstock.com; p. 22 Eric Isselee/Shutterstock.com.

Library of Congress Cataloging-in-Publication Data

Names: Klatte, Kathleen A., author.
Title: Owls at night / Kathleen A. Klatte.
Description: New York : PowerKids Press, [2021] | Series: Up all night!
   nocturnal animals | Includes index.
Identifiers: LCCN 2019047635 | ISBN 9781725318731 (paperback) | ISBN
   9781725318755 (library binding) | ISBN 9781725318748 (6 pack)
Subjects: LCSH: Owls—Juvenile literature. | Nocturnal animals—Juvenile
   literature.
Classification: LCC QL696.S8 K53 2021 | DDC 598.9/7—dc23
LC record available at https://lccn.loc.gov/2019047635

Some of the images in this book illustrate individuals who are models. The depictions do not imply actual situations or events.

Manufactured in the United States of America

CPSIA Compliance Information: Batch #CSPK20. For Further Information contact Rosen Publishing, New York, New York at 1-800-237-9932.

# CONTENTS

# WHO'S THERE?

Humans tend to make noise—even when we're trying very hard to be quiet. An owl sitting in a tree across the street could easily hear you moving around in your yard. Owls have excellent hearing.

Owls are raptors, or birds that hunt other animals. Most owls are nocturnal, which means they hunt at night. Other owls are crepuscular. This means they hunt at sunset. A few kinds of owls hunt during the day.

THIS OWL EASILY HEARD THE **RODENT** MOVING AROUND. ITS SOFT FEATHERS HELPED IT FLY SILENTLY AND COLLECT ITS DINNER. THE RODENT PROBABLY DIDN'T HEAR IT COMING.

Owls are covered in long, soft feathers. Some owls have tufts of feathers on their head that look like ears or horns. The feathers that cover an owl's ears are very fine so they can let sound in.

# OWLS AROUND THE WORLD

Owls live on every continent except Antarctica. There are about 180 kinds of owls. Elf owls are the smallest kind. They'e only about 6 inches (15.2 cm) long. Two of the largest owls are the great gray owl and the great horned owl. These owls' wings can measure 5 feet (1.5 m) from tip to tip.

Owls have **adapted** to many different types of **habitats**. They live and hunt in forests, grasslands, and even places where people live. Their coloring often blends into their surroundings. Being able to hide in plain sight makes it easier to hunt.

## WHILE YOU'RE SLEEPING

Modern owls are about the same size as modern hawks. However, there are fossils from much larger owls, some of which didn't even fly!

THIS GREAT HORNED OWL HAS MADE A HOME IN THIS TREE. LOOK HOW CLOSELY ITS FEATHERS MATCH THE TREE BARK.

# NIGHT BIRDS

Most owls live and hunt in darkness. Their big eyes take in all the light around them. This lets owls see in dim light, such as moonlight. Owls can't turn their eyes in their heads as people do. However, they can turn their heads nearly all the way around to get a view of their surroundings. Owls often see **prey** that can't see them.

Owls also use their hearing to find prey. The feathers that circle an owl's face direct sounds to the bird's ears. Owls can often pinpoint the location of prey by sound.

THE EARS OF MANY TYPES OF OWLS ARE PLACED ASYMMETRICALLY ON THEIR HEAD. THIS MEANS THAT ONE EAR IS HIGHER THAN THE OTHER. THIS HELPS THEM TO **FOCUS** ON THE SOUNDS AROUND THEM.

# SILENT GLIDERS

Owls are strong, silent hunters. They have large wings that they don't need to flap often. The feathers on these wings have soft edges, which quiet the sound of air moving through them. Their big, soft wings let owls fly without making any noise. This means owls can get near their prey without ever being heard.

Owls catch many kinds of prey. Many owls catch mice. Some owls eat fish and frogs. The smallest owls eat bugs and worms. Bigger owls eat small animals, such as rodents and rabbits, or other kinds of birds.

## WHILE YOU'RE SLEEPING

An owl's legs are very strong. Its feet have large, curved **talons**. This helps it grasp its prey and fly away with it.

OWLS ARE PREDATORS. THEIR EYES ARE SET IN THE FRONT OF THEIR FACES, ALLOWING THEM TO FOCUS ON THE MOVEMENTS OF TINY ANIMALS ON THE GROUND AS THEY FLY HIGH ABOVE.

# OWLS ON THE HUNT

Owls have different styles of hunting. Some owls fly quietly over the ground looking for food. Others sit on low branches to watch and listen for prey.

Once an owl discovers prey, it dives down and catches the animal in its talons. Then, the owl lifts the prey to its beak, which is curled down to help the bird hold its food. These raptors often swallow their prey whole.

ALTHOUGH IT'S NOT A GOOD IDEA TO PICK UP AN OWL PELLET YOU'VE FOUND OUTSIDE, SOME COMPANIES SELL PELLETS THAT HAVE BEEN **SANITIZED**. PEOPLE CAN PICK THE PELLETS APART TO SEE WHAT KINDS OF ANIMALS THE OWL HAS BEEN EATING.

Several hours after they've finished eating, owls spit up balls of bones, fur, and other things that their bodies can't break down. These are called pellets. They can sometimes be found under trees where owls live.

# AT HOME WITH OWLS

Many types of owls find places to live instead of building their own nests. They often live in dead trees, caves, and barns. Some owls live in the old nests of other large birds, such as crows.

Many owls have brown spots on their feathers. This makes the birds in their shadowy nests hard to see and keeps them safe during the day.

Owls make many sounds. They hoot, scream, and click their beaks. Each kind of owl has its own song. Owls use sounds and songs to talk with other owls. They make sounds to attract mates or to talk with their young.

## WHILE YOU'RE SLEEPING

European starlings are an **invasive species** that's moved into desert habitats in Mexico and the southwestern United States. They take nesting places from owls and other birds that are native to the area.

OWLS HAVE ADAPTED TO BEING AROUND PEOPLE IN TOWNS AND CITIES. THEY'LL NEST AND RAISE YOUNG INSIDE BUILDINGS IF THERE'S A SUITABLE OPENING.

# NESTS AND EGGS

Owls lay their eggs so that their babies will grow up at the time of year when the most food is available. Their eggs are round and white. Most mother owls lay three or four eggs at a time, though some owls lay up to 12 eggs. Mothers stay at their nests, keeping the eggs warm. Father owls bring the mothers food.

Baby owls are called chicks. Newly hatched owl chicks can't see and are covered with thick white **down**. As the babies grow, they get new feathers. After four to 10 weeks, the chicks start flying. If there isn't enough food for the entire brood, only the strongest and largest chicks will survive.

THIS BABY OWL DOESN'T HAVE ITS FLIGHT FEATHERS YET. ITS FEATHERS ARE SOFTER AND FUZZIER THAN ITS PARENTS' FEATHERS. IT DOES HAVE COLORING LIKE A GROWN OWL TO HELP IT BLEND IN WITH ITS SURROUNDINGS.

# BIG OWLS

The great horned owl is one of the most familiar owls to many people. It lives in deserts, forests, and cliffs all over North America and South America. The great horned owl gets its name from the tufts of feathers on its head. These large owls may be 2 feet (0.6 m) long and can weigh 5 pounds (2.3 kg). Great horned owls are brown with a bib of white feathers. They have large yellow eyes.

## WHILE YOU'RE SLEEPING

These big owls are known for their call. It sounds like "whoo whoo." Males have a larger voice box than females, which makes their voices deeper. You can hear the difference in **pitch** between a male and female.

GREAT HORNED OWLS HAVE VERY LARGE, POWERFUL FEET THAT THEY USE TO CATCH LARGE PREY ANIMALS. IT CAN TAKE 28 POUNDS (12.7 KG) OF FORCE TO OPEN A GREAT HORNED OWL'S TALONS ONCE THEY ARE CLOSED.

Great horned owls hunt mostly at night. They eat rabbits, skunks, and many other animals. They can catch other large raptors. Their fierce grip can cut the spine of their prey.

# LITTLE OWLS

People often identify owls by their calls. Northern saw-whet owls even get their name from their call. Male northern saw-whets make a call that sounds like "skiew." This reminds some people of a saw being whetted, or sharpened, and may be the origin of their name.

Northern saw-whet owls live in forests in the United States, southern Canada, and central Mexico. At night, the owls hunt for little animals such as mice. These small owls are generally between 7 and 8.5 inches (17.8 and 21.6 cm) long. Like other kinds of owls, males of the species, or kind, are smaller.

NORTHERN SAW-WHET OWLS ARE ABOUT THE SIZE OF ROBINS. THEY'RE SO TINY THAT AN ADULT MOUSE CAN LAST THEM FOR TWO MEALS.

# PEOPLE AND OWLS

Owls have featured in human **culture** since at least the time of the ancient Greeks. In the past, people thought these birds had magical powers. Some believed owls brought bad luck. Other people thought owls were wise. Today, we know that owls aren't magic.

However, these wonderful birds are helpful to us. For example, owls eat animals, such as mice and rats, that eat crops and bother people. We can help owls by not poisoning the rats they eat. We can also build boxes in trees for owls to use as nests. Preserving the wild places where they live will also help make sure that owls have a safe future.

# GLOSSARY

**adapt:** To change in order to live better in a certain environment.

**culture:** The beliefs and ways of life of a certain group of people.

**down:** A covering of soft fluffy feathers.

**focus:** To direct attention at.

**habitat:** The natural home for plants, animals, and other living things.

**invasive species:** Plants or animals from one area that spread quickly in a new area and harm native plants and animals.

**pitch:** The highness or lowness of a sound.

**prey:** An animal hunted by other animals for food.

**rodent:** A small, furry animal with large front teeth, such as a mouse or rat.

**sanitize:** To make something free from dirt, sickness, etc., by cleaning it.

**talon:** One of the sharp claws on the feet of some birds.

# INDEX

# WEBSITES

Due to the changing nature of Internet links, PowerKids Press has developed an online list of websites related to the subject of this book. This site is updated regularly. Please use this link to access the list: www.powerkidslinks.com/uan/owls